I Touch the Earth,

The Earth

Touches Me

I Touch the Earth,
The Earth
Touches Me

Hugh Prather

Illustrations by Paul Kinslow

Doubleday & Company, Inc.

Garden City, New York

ISBN: 0-385-05063-1
Library of Congress Catalog Card Number 72–79420
Copyright © 1972 by Hugh Prather
Printed in the United States of America
All Rights Reserved

15   14   13   12   11   10

For Gayle
(who is the only rabbit)

Foreword

This book, like the one which preceded it, evolved. It is taken from a notebook that I write in from time to time, and includes the last two to three years of my life. The entries I have selected are in chronological order, at least in terms of internal time, if not external, and taken as a whole I believe that they exhibit the same curious pattern I saw in my last book: that every time I think that I have learned something, my life seems to deliberately set about contradicting it. Yet the contradiction is never absolute; it is more a quarter turn than a whole. And so I am left with this belief: that there are no answers, there are only alternatives, and the best that I can do is trust my present experience and follow where it leads me. —And it has led me down some amazingly divergent paths, from Mary Baker Eddy to Fritz Perls, from Maxwell Maltz to Krishnamurti . . . but somehow, at the time, each one worked, each one was needed, and, conversely, each of them became poison to me when I inevitably clung to their words in spite of my experience.

So I want to remind you that every entry in this book is at best an asymptotic shot at life, and at my life, not at yours. If my words affirm you, then savor them for the moment; but if they cause you to distrust your own experience, spit them out. You are the only authority on what is good for you, and once you have seen this, you will feel an enormous peace and freedom.

soft the sky

fills

and softly

spills

soft the drop

drips

gently down

and soft my foot

falls

soft the ground

and down the ground

fills

gently down

There is a flat way of seeing; I know it well; I live with
it most of the day. And there is a spiritual way of
seeing which comes to me suddenly, and when it does that
day is rare. With this new vision I can see the innocence
woven through all men and things, as though a shaft of light
had fallen across treasured objects in a forgotten closet,
and for a moment I live with this vision, and I and all things
around me are changed.

I associate this spiritual way of seeing with many causes:
with music and poetry, with sunsets and seas, with friends
who are friends, with love, and now and then with a book or
a passage within a book. These things have at times
inspired me to this broader vision, but rarely have I
been able to return and use one of them to recapture it.
If I try, the poem or song will have lost its magic, and I
only receive an echo of my previous wonder.

Sometimes I doubt and sometimes I believe. And I like not making myself believe when I am doubting, and not making myself doubt when I am believing. Surely neither God nor Accident need my consistency.

When I paint I am influenced by the texture of the paper,
the viscosity of the paint, the condition of the brush.
I reach down to make a thin line and it comes out plump.
Then the picture takes a new direction—I influencing it;
it influencing me.

I start to do one thing and something else happens "to
divert me." I resent the influence and try to go back to
my original intention. But I *am* influenced. I am ever
influenced. I do not live in a vacuum together with my
intentions. I am a relationship. I walk down the road
and feel a sudden burst of warmth from the sun: I stop and
bask my eyes. I get a letter from John, a nibble from Rufus,
a knowing look from a clerk and I am no longer the same.
What I just was doesn't quite apply. What I just intended
is in the past. This is not a lack of resolve, it is the
way life flows: always a new painting, always a new me.

Am I more a mind than a body, more a body than a feeling, more a feeling than a memory, more a memory than a future? Sometimes I am all anger and sometimes all peace. There are minutes I live for tomorrow and minutes I live for her. In last night's hot bed I was flesh and afterward I was soul. But most moments I am not just a body, or a mind, and when I am at peace with this reality and my intellect does not override my flesh and my here does not deny my tomorrow, and when emotions and memories and needs and all the et cetera of my being each has its voice, I can see that I am how everyone else is . . . and possibly even how every*thing* is.

Cause and effect have no stopping point. Everything
I do touches everything else. Since I have become more
willing to express my displeasure I notice that I have
started crossing my t's. And somehow this is related
to the comment I made recently about Beulah: "She
liked me until I crossed her." And all of this appears
to accompany my new posture: I no longer hold my head
down as much. And I suspect there are a thousand
other connections.

I do not see growth as a procedure which locates "the real me"; I look at it more as a process whereby I become aware of other aspects of myself which are equally as "real" as the familiar me. I am always "being real" to some part of my personality and, at that moment, not "being real" to other parts. In this sense I am always acting, always choosing to act out a particular side of me. There is no such state as "not in touch." Everyone is in touch with something. There is the state of being *out* of touch—out of touch with areas of my body, with nature, with other people, with other aspects of my personality. And there is such a state as being stuck in what I am in touch with. Much of my life I have been aware of my intellect and little else. And this is true of most of the people I know: they stay pretty much within one chamber of their being.

When Buz stayed with us I noticed that 80% of his conversation was about "Great People I Have Known or Read About." I wonder if most people's conversation centers mainly on a single theme. John's appears to be "Interesting Facts About the World Around Us." Beulah's is "Enlightening Experiences I Have Had." Mine is "Insightful Ideas in Psychology."

No matter what we talk about, we are talking about ourselves.

My attitude toward much of life is habitual: I have a fairly consistent telephone personality, a different but predictable party personality and I make about the same kind of supermarket customer every time. I am in approximately the same mood each time I brush my teeth, run an errand, meet somebody or take a crap. I pick out what I am going to wear beginning with my shirt, seldom with my pants, and I shave starting with my chin. I never jump with joy in the shower or act silly while driving. I am mildly good humored when I wake up and never precipitously go to bed. All of these attitudes feel "right" and veering from them feels "phony." I guess it could be said that I am being "genuine," but genuinely what?

I feel as if I am slowly dying when my life is in a rut,
but my attitude toward ritual is more affirmative. I have a
friend whose ritual is popcorn and beer. It begins every
evening after his wife has gone to bed. He fixes his
popcorn to perfection, sits in front of the fireplace,
then his dog lies beside him and receives the first two bites.
A relative of mine has a morning ritual of eating breakfast
and feeding birds from his large porch while he telephones
his friends one by one to say good morning. My ritual
revolves around taking an afternoon nap. I have certain
trivial things that I do each time before I get into bed,
and, although there are many days that I do not nap, when I
do I enjoy going about it in a familiar way.

In order to break with a habit I will first have to become aware of how I *usually* act. I will have to see how I do it before I can undo it. At the time, I am not aware of how I shut down my attention or hold back my warmth.

When I am going to sleep or waking up I have noticed that
certain areas of my body feel drowsy while others feel
stimulated, and that if I want to sleep I can generally
do so by fixing my attention on the drowsy parts. It
may be that this same principle applies to attitudes.
When I check to see how I feel about something, I
automatically move my attention to the region of my
solar plexus. But it appears that there are other aspects
of my personality which are centered in quite different
areas of my body. Tonight when I explored these I found
that from my back I was strong and stolid, from my feet
I felt athletic and slightly impatient, and from my
hands I was cool, liquid and glib. In my neck, eyes and
shoulders there were still other differences. The
question, "How do I feel about this?" might be answered,
"Feel from where?" In this way I could not deceive myself
into believing that I have only one attitude to which I
can be true.

I think of the process of "being real" as the shuttling of
my attention between a feeling and an appearance, between
inside and acting-out. But "being real" does not mean that
I am only allowed to shuttle between my behavior and my
strongest feeling. My behavior can match whatever in me
I wish it to match. "Being real" is simply being aware of
what my actions do in fact match. To think that I must always
behave in accord with what I feel *most* is self-reduction,
whereas at any moment I am free to act on any dimly
felt and long-neglected part of me: to be a ham, to be
strong, to flirt, to cry, to be totally silly, to dance,
to play peek-a-boo or stick out my tongue. And if
this feels phony because it has been so long since I have
responded to this in me, still it is not phony; it is me;
I am doing it.

Humor is a way of relating to people that I feel uncomfortable with. I am more familiar with what it takes to be serious.

I am admitting that I want something when I try to be funny. I do not require as much co-operation in order to be serious. Humor comes more easily when I am around people I don't feel I need anything from.

When I try hard to be funny I am small and gray, but when I am easy with myself, and allow other people's fun to sparkle through me, and allow my own lightness to roll gently out of me, then good humor rhymes in all the sweet times around me.

If I hold back any part of me I suppress that much energy and potential. The question that I want to ask myself now is not what behavior is "good" or "bad," but in what ways would I express myself with great energy if I didn't hold back. How much energy would there be if I did what I think of as putting people down, or seducing, or being a know-it-all? I suspect that the qualities I consider ugly are simply ones in which I have not yet allowed my entire force, that if I would express these traits honestly, they might ripen into something full-flavored and whole.

For months I have been fighting my nice-guy game, but today I consciously used it. Gayle and I were sneaking onto the St. John's tennis courts when two professors drove up. I went over to them, said hello, commented on the wind, asked if they had seen yesterday's Ashe-Newcomb match and sought their advice on yellow tennis balls. The result was that not only did Gayle and I get to play tennis but that I felt much stronger, much more centered, than when I have slipped into this game out of fear. There was something honest about being *consciously* dishonest: I took responsibility for my actions.

How would I act if I *didn't* feel inept when Dave is being hilarious? How would I write if I *could* write like James Joyce? How would I greet Bob if I *weren't* reserved? How would I look at a woman if I *did* think I was sexy? How would I act if I could act any way I wanted to? How would I be if I weren't tired or fat or scared or blocked or whatever it is I am always telling myself?

This morning I let out the long-suppressed Dale Carnegie side of me when I ran into Jim. I had only met him once and really like him. He lit up at my enthusiastic niceness and invited me to dinner—which is just what I had hoped he would do.

What would I discover about the cottonwoods if when I walked
to the mailbox I listened to them instead of looked at
them? What would I find out about the rain if I didn't run
inside? And is it possible that a sunrise would refresh
me more than sleep?

Tonight at dinner I tried picking up my glass with my
left hand instead of my right and didn't feel quite so
self-assured. It was a nice feeling.

Almost every small boy whom I have seen walking down the corridor at the airport runs his hands along the deliciously tiled wall.

There were seventy-five people in the lobby and only a seven-year-old girl was finding out what it felt like to sit on a marble floor.

It's this simple: If I never try anything, I never learn anything. If I never take a risk, I stay where I am.

If I go ahead and do it, that affects how much I continue wanting to do it.

When I hold myself back, I trade appearances for the opportunity to find out what I am like.

I say that I accept the way I am, but do I accept it so fully that I am willing to act on it—to actually *act* the way I am?

I have to act the way I am now before I can become something else.

I agree with Nelson: "We can't change, but we can expand."

This Christmas, Norman said, "I have known you since the third grade. I have seen you as a Christian Scientist, a vegetarian, an avid businessman, and now this, whatever it is.
Your ideas change, but you always remain the same."

I am not sure if I have changed either. I know that today
I am a little more aware of my body, a little more aware
of nature, a little more aware of other people . . . but that's
not really "changed," it's more "returned"—returned to
some of what I started this life with. And I also know
that I am a little more tolerant of the way I am, and of the
way other people are (those two things usually go together).
And I know that I have a few more alternatives now,
I am able to respond in some ways that I couldn't a few
years ago. I think Norman is probably right—only ideas
change. I have read about saints and high people, but
I have never known one. Awareness and tolerance and
openness don't seem to really change me, they just allow me.

He called tonight. He's going to be a big-time politician, he says; and he probably will. As I listened to him I said to myself, "There is a real live human being under all of that."

You say you want "to be somebody"—then apparently you don't want to be yourself.

Fame isn't fame: it only appears that way from a distance.

There is nothing to *achieve*
There *is* nothing to achieve
There is *nothing* to achieve

As long as my attention stays fixed on how well *Notes* is doing I will remain where I am. Ambition is having the opposite effect of "getting me ahead"; it is keeping me stuck. Ambition is an extension of the past. It is a desire for more of something already known. *Openness* is what will "get me ahead," because openness does not know what is ahead—it has no rigid idea of what is needed.

If all my striving, planning, rehearsing came true, this would only give me a bigger version of myself. Real progress can't be imagined. I can't anticipate in thought what new vision life will lay before me or in which direction it will next demand my growth.

"I wish" assumes that I know what is the opposite of my present experience.

"A promising young man" is a hole yet to be filled. Thought won't fill it. To stop this clatter in my head I will have to die to the future; I will have to give up "having promise."

open

and alert

empty

and available

human and

alive

waiting

(without purpose)

ready

(without wanting)

existing

(without needing)

I parked the car in front of the post office and Don and
I got out. I got out *to go to the post office*. Then I
realized that Don had gotten out, was walking and noticing,
and was only *heading* toward the post office.

Gayle and I took Natasha to meet my parents. When we got
out of the car and started toward the door, I was in a state
and Gayle was in a state but Natasha was fascinated with the
shrubbery.

Walking without a goal (to get somewhere)
Eating without a goal (to get full)
Looking without a goal (to judge)
Talking without a goal (to convince)
Living without a goal (to accomplish)

There is no harm in wanting to accomplish; the harm
is in *having* to accomplish.

My desire to accomplish is as periodic as my desire
for meat, and when I have it nothing else satisfies me
except hard work and a job done with care.

I spend an inordinate amount of time looking for
something to *do*, looking for *ways* to become whole,
when all the while my organism, God, or whatever one wants
to call it, is ticking away and all I need do is stay
with the rhythm.

A problem does not have to be thought about in order
to be solved.

Sometimes when I am scared I like to turn on the light.

What *should* I do?

Nothing
Nothing is the thing to do
(Nothing is the only doing)

I am worthwhile just existing
("Just"? —OK, I am worthwhile
existing)

What if the stars were to start doing something?
("What are you doing hummingbird?"
"I'm just being a hummingbird"
"Oh, is *that* all?")

As soon as I start doing
I stop being

"I don't understand how you do so little."
(Now *that's* a compliment)

Not opening a can of tuna because last night's roast
will spoil if I don't eat it; not changing the thermostat
because later it might get too hot; not pulling over the
coffee table to eat on because I will have to put it back—
I am surprised at how much I indenture myself to the future.

Making my bed, putting up the toothpaste—my perfectionism
centers me in the future.

Whenever I stand up, sit down, start to walk, start to reach, my attention jumps out of the present and I become temporarily absent from my body. Having a goal, even one so small as getting a glass of water, does not require that I leave my senses. I can know what I want to do and still remain present.

The question is not whether to have goals. The question is whether it's a goal *now* or a goal *then*.

Struggling to make her reach a climax is just as much working for a goal as struggling to reach one myself. If I am having sex in *her* future I am still not having sex *now*.

Staying with the rhythm of the sanding, watching the wood slide into creamy richness, doing it to be doing it and not just to have it done.

It makes no sense to hurry up, and so mess up, what I am doing now in order to get started on what I plan to do next.

Every moment that I am centered in the future I suffer a temporary loss of this life.

It's not that "today is the first day of the rest of my life," but that *now* is all there is of my life.

The paradox of progress is that I grow each time I realize that I can only be where I am.

My growth does not seem to be a matter of learning new lessons, but of learning the old lessons again and again. The wisdom doesn't change, only the situations.

Another kind of "being in touch": being in touch with the
situation, being open to the signal that "enough is enough."
Events are not controlled by my will. It is irrelevant
how I *want* things to go; the question is, how are they
going. "I want this marriage to work out"—but *is it*
working out?

Surely this must be an ancient proverb: If the situation
is killing you, get the hell out.

The black stinch of that accident today and the desperate red flailing. And then I saw all that yellow gas bellying down on California—and here I am just taking it like all the rest of these miserable people. Awareness can become a nightmare, and right now it is too much for me. All I want is to slowly sink my head into soft boredom and trivia.

For the last three weeks I have been very comfortable with a routine. It has been a nice socially acceptable way to take a nap.

Problems do not choose me. "Me against you," "Me against it" comes with my having a path. But *life* is not the single lane. All the lanes are in me. I can look back now and see how so many of my difficulties resulted from the one-eyed way I chose to march.

How I am working on a problem often indicates how I am keeping it a problem.

So often I wrestle with myself over how I *want* to feel instead of trying to discover how I *really* feel.

I didn't realize until today just how powerful is my fear of being thought stupid. I went into a bookstore and the owner asked me to inscribe some books. As I was writing in one of them I suddenly came to a word I couldn't spell. Ironically, the word was "controlled." "Does it have one 'l' or two? If I spell it wrong they will see it as soon as I leave . . . but if I ask, all these people standing around will . . ." At that point I literally broke out in a sweat.

Beautiful women usually scare me, especially tall blondes.
I feel slightly inadequate whenever I meet one. If I really
like her I seem to do everything possible to indicate
that I have no interest: I don't look in her eyes
unless I have to; I act very innocent and polite; and if
her boyfriend or husband is with her I direct most of
my comments to him.

"I feel apprehensive." —"Apprehensive" is an interpretation.
What I *feel* is a sensation.

This is so important: not to think that I have to always
do something about the sensations which go off in my body,
not to think that I have to give them names and plan immediate
action—instead, to look at sorrow "without the word," to
look at hunger "without the word," to feel what I feel
without forcing connections with the past or projecting
future consequences.

I don't have to be sexually aroused *for* something.
Simply being aroused is often pure pleasure.

One evening, shortly after I had met a famous therapist,
I asked her if she would work with me on a chronic stomach
problem. She answered that she never worked in the
evenings. It had taken a considerable effort for me to ask,
and when I heard her words I felt a hot charge move from
my chest to my head. Although I haven't always done this
before, this time I just stayed with the sensations; I
didn't jump from them to thoughts about the therapist.
After a few moments the sensations dissolved and the
whole matter was finished. There was no hurt still
lingering on sentences in my head.

Gayle has just taken in another cat . . . to look at cats without the name . . . to look at *these* cats without saying the number . . . to know what I want to do about this situation, rather than about how it will appear.

To eat an egg "without the word." To notice *this*: how it looks, how it tastes, how I feel with it inside me.

Today I was leaving a very small store, weaving my way through the people standing near the door, when the owner suddenly called out, "That's the author!" I immediately went blind with self-consciousness and could see almost nothing until I got out the door. Before the owner spoke, the people I was trying to get through meant nothing to me, but the moment after her announcement they became very important. I was interested in seeing their reaction, but I didn't show it, and I felt intensely looked at. I don't know if I *was* looked at, I just *felt* looked at. I am beginning to see that I only feel looked at by people whom I am interested in, and that the feeling of being looked at isn't as strong if I don't hold myself back from looking.

Almost any difficulty will move in the face of honesty. When I am honest I never feel stupid. And when I am honest I am automatically humble.

Whether it is writing a book, painting a picture or furnishing a room, I do not believe that a person can do it *his way* without being creative.

A lie can sometimes save a great amount of energy. And sometimes so can not telling a lie.

"But you couldn't be sleepy, you had nine hours sleep."

"But you couldn't be hungry, you just finished eating."

"But you couldn't be sick, you just had a checkup."

"But you couldn't be depressed, you just got a new car."

"But you couldn't be bruised, I didn't hit you that hard."

(Dishonesty is a state in which I am mesmerized by my words and disregard my senses.)

I am amazed at how many "secrets" I have been able to let go of since this one incident: I told Dave that there was a phone in the bedroom if ever he didn't want to use the one in the living room. He paused a moment, then said, "I don't believe I have anything I want to hide."

If I want to talk to someone and I am stuck for something to say, one of the simplest ways for me to get started is to state honestly what I am experiencing: "I want very much to talk to you but no words are coming."

If I'm rehearsing it, isn't it obvious that I want to
do it?

As long as I am trying to decide, I can't *feel* what I
want to do.

One reason that I sometimes have difficulty "deciding"
is that I assume that I should have no reservations.
The word itself implies a completion. Often I can
bypass "deciding" simply by noticing in which direction
I am leaning. Asking myself, "What is my preference?"
cuts through this perfectionism.

If I do what I prefer rather than what I have "decided,"
then I am a little more open to change: I do not have
to think my way back through to a new conclusion; I
simply notice what it is I prefer *now*.

There are many things that I can do a little of at the
very moment I find myself thinking, "How awful that I
haven't been doing that." I suspect it is no coincidence
that my self-criticism comes right at the time that I
can do something about it.

When my day is going poorly, I keep on muttering through
it "until I have time," instead of stopping right then and
bringing myself together.

By approaching my problems with "What might make things a little better?" rather than "What is the solution?" I avoid setting myself up for certain frustration. My experience has shown me that I am not going to solve anything in one stroke; at best I am only going to chip away at it.

The word "problem" implies an illusion: that this trouble I am having has definable limits. —Everything runs into everything else.

I buy things I don't need, then look for ways to use them in order to justify the purchase—in this way I end up doing what I don't want to *twice*.

Today a friend wrote me, "Do you think you *are* a mistake just because you made one?"

There is no such thing as a mistake. There is only what happens.

My day has become a fraction happier ever since I realized
that nothing is *exactly* the way I would like it to be.
This is simply the way life is—and there goes one battle
I don't have to fight any more.

Today I heard an old woman say, "Whatever I worry about is
not worth worrying about."

I'm glad I heard that.

I see that I have made rules for myself about certain words,
words such as "why," "how," "is," "feel," "because," "should."
But there are no taboo words, no should or shouldn't words,
no rules. It's not words, but what may be happening inside
me when I use certain words. All I need is to be alert to
what *is* happening, to look where the word is coming from.
If I am weighing my words, I am being somebody else.
If I don't say what I say, I am an appearance.

I like what Warren McCulloch said: "Don't bite my finger,
look where I am pointing."

There are no rules, no shoulds, no
have-to's . . .
I am free.

There are no rules, no shoulds, no
have-to's . . .
I am free.

There are no rules, no shoulds, no
have-to's . . .
I am free.

"Growth" can get to be such a deadly business.

I saw Dina at the party tonight. She smiled brightly and said, "This year I decided to give up suffering."

I am weary of hearing therapists compare therapies. Why this eternal need to debunk? Isn't it obvious by now that just as it was true of any religion, so too any therapy which makes a man's life happier is good for *him*?

I believe that a therapy is just one way of seeing. It is an emphasis and as such neglects everything else. A new therapy has at times helped me feel clearer about one or two situations that the old ones didn't, but no therapy has ever seemed to quite fit my life. At least I have never found a written statement, religious, therapeutic or otherwise, which has dealt with anything in my life *exactly*.

I see a number of my friends tormenting themselves over the belief that they can (and therefore should) remove every last trace of some "block" or "impasse." These terms, like the expression "work through," imply the existence of the other side ("completion," "finished situation," "completed transaction," etc.). More and more I am doubting the helpfulness of such a view. What I choose to see as a problem can always be looked at differently. Even among therapies, what one therapy views as someone's "block" another sees as his sign of health. I doubt that it is possible to completely work through such universally held states as anxiety and phobia, although it is clearly possible to move in the direction of greater freedom. I do not even know someone I see as having *completely* worked through a bitter and chronic resentment, and when I have thought that *I* have done so, a trace of it will surface and remind me that the human brain does not erase so easily. I am at the place now where if I believe that something in me is disturbing my enjoyment of life, I will work on it for awhile (for as long as working on it feels good), but I am losing my zeal for "completion."

Getting out is getting in
Going in is getting through
(Around is not through)

"I am here" is getting there
"Wish I were there" is staying here
(Moving is standing very still)

Having is getting
Wanting is not receiving
(Being is very filling)

There is still a taboo against having a good time. Somehow life is not supposed to be fun. I have thirty or forty years left, or maybe it's thirty or forty seconds, and I believe that enjoying this time may be the *only* thing that really matters.

When I was playing tennis with Nelson this afternoon he said, "As I have been going from one activity to another today I have been asking myself, 'Is this what I am alive for?'"

Self-discipline ceases to feel like internal warfare whenever I see that, given the alternatives which I have allowed myself, I am always doing what I want to do.

There is a kind of trying which affirms me, as when our kitten tries again and again to climb a tree until she has succeeded. And there is a sick kind of trying which denies me, as when I try to make someone like me and become less and less with each failure. When I try in this way I am looking outward at a wish or ideal, and so I am turned away from noticing me.

At times it seems that all of my thinking is an effort to become. My thoughts say in effect: "Look at the past, you certainly did that well" (i.e., be more like that in the future) or "Look what happened, you sure made a fool of yourself" (don't be like that again) or "Take what you're experiencing now, for example; here's how you could use it to your advantage" (in the future).

Most thoughts are jottings on a memo pad which will never be used.

This afternoon my friend, Ray, read what I had written
about listening with my eyes to the stars and said, "Oh
I get it, you play the feminine, the yin, and let nature
play the masculine, the yang." —When you conceptualize
it, Ray, you bury it.

As long as I am thinking I am not fully present.

Jerry told me he was disturbed that his drawings of women always looked sinister. When he added that he often used pictures in *Playboy* to draw from, I said that it was understandable that his drawings looked sinister because these women were acting so phony. Now I wish I hadn't said that. I gave him an explanation. If he accepted it he may now be further away from discovering something about himself than he was before. He wanted to look inside himself and I held up some damned explanation for him to look at.

Thinking is a symptom.

That fear perpetuates much of my thinking is obvious to me: fear that I might not become.

Filling my head with thoughts sometimes gives me the illusion of not being alone.

As soon as I take my attention off my mind it starts up again. This has been going on for two weeks. I want to clear my mind but it is obvious that I can't go about it this way.
(Well, why do you want to clear your mind?
So that I can see the world around me.
OK, then start seeing the world around you!)

Trying to stop all thinking is like looking into one mirror reflecting another mirror. To get free of the whirl I have to step into my senses.

But isn't the goal to stop all thinking simply thought battling thought?

And if I attempt to eliminate *all* thinking, aren't I condemning it? And if I condemn it, how can I see it as anything but bad?

I don't want silence as a rule. What I want is the *alternative* of a silent mind.

There are other ways of thinking besides the circular, half-aware prattling that makes up most of the conversation in my head. I sometimes use words to work my way through confusion: to unwind, to untangle. These words create direction. And there is that state in meditation when occasional thoughts flicker gently in and out of my mind like birds on wing or shooting stars. And there is another kind of thought which speaks directly from the core of me, a sudden seeing with words . . . and still I am not certain that the words are necessary. I suspect that they are not the seeing, they may only be my echoing of the seeing; and some day, some day very far away, I may be able to put aside all words, like a child puts aside his tracing.

I believe that when my dad (Hugh Prather, Jr.) wrote
this poem, he must have been remembering what it was
like to live for a moment without thought:

It was cold and still at night
Stars like lanterns hanging bright
Endless skies with silver tones
Reaching down beyond my mind
Feeling more than what I was
My spirit soaring out beyond
Knowing I could do it now
No matter what the world had said.

Seeing groups of starlit forms
Moving thru some unknown power
Believing I could touch the real
Now that time would pass me by.

Endless worlds were opening up
Colors, forms, unknown before
Chromatic tones of harmony

Words no longer seemed of use
Old ways of thinking left behind
Images clear as sunlit dew
Flowing freely thru my mind
Being as the image formed
Without space and time between.

Looking back it seemed a dream
Only now was real to me
The depth and feeling of its force
Moving me beyond myself.

One way of looking at a fantasy is to notice what it does for me physically, what it triggers in my body, how it changes my behavior, such as the fantasies I use to get to sleep, or the ones I use to become sexually aroused. All of these may be of some benefit; but what about the fantasies I use to keep myself angry over an incident already past, or the ones I use to stop me from taking a reasonable risk?

Sometimes fantasies are reminders of unfinished business. Sometimes they are my defense against taking action. Sometimes fantasies are an attempt on the part of my organism to make me more aware of some feeling I am neglecting. Sometimes they are the indirect means I use to criticize myself. Sometimes fantasies are my way of producing a wanted emotion. Sometimes they are my proposed goals. But fantasies are always *fantasies*, and no matter what the subject, I am fantasizing about myself.

Sometimes if I can look at a dream or fantasy *simply* enough, its meaning becomes clear.

Me: "There is something wrong with my life and I don't understand what it is."

Dream: "Look, I'll draw you a picture."

When I get a clear statement about my life from a dream, it is usually contained more in the emotions than in what I see. The visual part of the dream often appears to be a representation of what I am feeling during the dream, the individual images being taken from situations in my life that have commonly surrounded those feelings. Usually they are feelings which I have had recently, especially that day, and they seem to always be ones that I brushed over. Seen in this way my dreams could be interpreted as saying, "Look what you were feeling today—you didn't fully acknowledge it."

These questions sometimes help me notice something that I wasn't seeing about a dream:

What are my emotions during the dream, what am I feeling or *not* feeling, and how are these emotions familiar?

What is the action of the dream pointing to; what does the action say needs to be done?

What does the dream say I am avoiding; what is *not* being said or done?

Where is the power in the dream; what is controlling?

What is missing in the dream; what would ordinarily be there that is not?

From where or what is a threat coming?

Does the dream stop short of something happening—what conclusion do I fantasize?

In what way does the dream say I frustrate myself; what comes in to thwart or change the course of action?

What is the mood (setting) of the dream, and how is my life like this mood?

I believe that dreams serve a useful function within my organism whether I do something with them or not. Most of my dreams do not have a clear, unforced meaning for me, and if the message does not become obvious to me quickly I usually drop working on it.

In order to see more clearly I have to take notice of what I can already see, rather than look for what I should be able to see but can't.

I don't have to *become* aware. I don't have to start seeing or even learn how to listen. My body is already aware. I already see. All I need is to be open to my awareness, remain conscious of what it is I am already seeing. Awareness is given and all that is required is to keep thought out of its way, which of course is not a doing, but a not-doing.

I hear many people today talking about "awareness" as if it were *the* solution. Awareness is a word, a word like "love" which has a very roomy definition—but not one roomy enough to include everything.

I don't *like* an alarm clock but it's useful to me. I
don't *like* tension but it tells me something needs
attending.

When Popi Da begins to anticipate our going for a run
he does a series of stretches, yawns and little squeals.
Moosewood and Depot acted exactly the same: as soon as
tension started flowing into their muscles they responded
by stretching and moving. For all these years I have
been reacting to excitement and tension by *tightening*
my muscles, by bottling it up, so as not to show it.

My body attempts to look, act and feel like what I put
into it. If in my imagination I hold up all the trash
I eat in one hand and hold up my body in the other,
what I am doing to myself becomes obvious.

How much tension have I pressed into my body, how much
have I strained to keep myself under control? Is it any
wonder that I am stiff after compressing myself inside
a vice for thirty-three years?

For several months
now I have been
stretching whatever
wants to be
stretched, making
up how I do it as
I go along, letting
my muscles and
joints tell me
what they need,
doing it whenever
and for as long
as it feels good.
The effect, especially
as compared to routine
body-tightening calisthenics,
is so mentally releasing
that I believe it
somehow nourishes
my psyche, just as eating
exactly what my stomach
tells me it wants
nourishes my flesh.

I think nothing of taking care of my stomach any time of the day that I get hungry; why not take care of my muscles right when they begin to get tight or tired?

This evening I finally did it: I stopped giving myself a headache. When I felt it coming on I stood very still, and let go of all the pushing—and for the rest of the evening my neck and head felt free.

Is my body the mirror of my psyche, and illness but an image?

I am beginning to see that most of my illnesses have been an externalization of an internal conflict, that my body gets sick whenever I am not letting go.

Allowing the pain to talk to me. *Listening* to the complaints of my body. Noticing what my ulcer forces me to do.

Tonight when my mother got mad at me I stood up and stretched my arms toward the ceiling, and when I sat down I found that I really had nothing to say to her.

While I was talking to my landlord this evening I noticed that, as usual, my mouth was open, and that, as usual, I was swallowing everything he was saying. Then I closed my mouth and found that I felt less like nodding, more like disagreeing.

Jan looked up while Rolfing my feet and said that they were sweating heavily. A few days later I noticed that I was only standing on one foot while talking to Barry Stevens.

Mike was here when Mother called. After I hung up he told me how he had finally gotten to the point where he could listen to *his* needs while his mother talked to him on the phone.

In what ways do I let people manipulate me? Through politeness? Through threatened anger? Through dangled sex? If someone is mildly abrupt with me, I usually respond in a predictable (controllable) way: I become A-REAL-NICE-GUY.

Getting hurt comes when I am acting too nice to risk hurting.

I think that jealousy comes when I have failed to use my own power, failed to take my own stand. I suspect that this is also behind my resentments.

The insanity in holding back my anger is that I am evidently more willing to risk destroying me than destroying a relationship.

I see that tensing my butt and taking shallow breaths go together. It is difficult for me to take a full abdominal breath and still maintain a tight butt. Now I want to see what will happen if I start breathing fully the next time I notice that I am holding myself back emotionally.

When Joe said that he wanted to make love to me, I got a sudden pain in the small of my back. This is the first time that I have seen clearly how I give myself back trouble.

I suspect that the overfullness of my body is related to
the underfullness of my voice: both appear to be ways
that I insulate myself from making contact.

Whenever I sit cross-legged my right knee will not go down
as far as my left one. This evening, when I was attending
the play, I noticed that I was holding my right knee up
so that it wouldn't touch the person sitting next to me.

Now I see the connection between my leaning over when
I walk and my not being open, my not letting people in.

How do I keep people out? What am I doing with my words, my eyes, to hold this person away? Am I letting his voice touch me, or am I only hearing it? Am I using my eyes to see him or to "look him in the eye?"

Letting people in is largely a matter of not expending the energy to keep them out.

I just noticed that I don't look at Popi Da when I pet him.

Some of the ways that I have kept myself out of touch with my body:

Consulting a clock to see if I have had enough sleep.

Trying to recall how much I have eaten in order to know how much I want to eat now.

Putting on glasses when my eyes hurt (instead of resting them).

Using aspirin and antacids.

Wearing loose clothes so that I won't feel the objectional contours of my body.

Putting thick soles and heels between me and the ground.

Breathing through my mouth (which has no sense of smell).

Using strong chemicals to prevent my body from perspiring and having its natural odor.

Never brushing up against a stranger in a crowd.

Holding myself back from touching people when I talk to them.

Not looking at the parts of another person's body that I want to look at.

Another kind of awareness:
awareness of the *activity*.
Getting into the rhythm
of walking. Really
walking—the whole
freely-flowing,
breathing,
swinging, stepping-out
and seeing-it-all-go-by
movement. Getting into
the rhythm of riding a bike,
doing dishes, running,
dancing, driving. Awareness
of the whole activity that
the body is engaged in,
as well as awareness of
the individual limbs and
their motions.

Relaxed muscles do not necessarily make relaxed movements. I have been relaxing my limbs, but my *walk* has remained stiff.

I have noticed that when I start trying I literally stick my neck out.

Effortless posture is not holding my body in position, but being in position where I am not holding.

As I lay in bed early this morning, too tired to get up but not tired enough to sleep, I thought how typical that moment was of most moments. All the old solutions weren't quite working, there were no apparent new ones, and as usual my modern commandment, "Become aware of how you are doing it," stunk with inadequacy. I spend so much of my time kidding myself that I know something. But there are so few moments when I really know what is going on, so very, very few.

Every time I think I know something, life keeps on being itself, and I am left standing on my head.

It seems as though the truth that is needed today is always a lie by tomorrow.

There are no "best ways." There are only alternatives.

One night I had an insight. Afterward I saw the same thing
again and again. Then there were other times when I didn't
see it, I only said it. If I see something I have never
seen before, afterward I am more alert to this new way of
looking. But this pattern is not the accumulation of
knowledge, because each time I have to see it. If the next
time I only apply the idea, if I only say the words, then
seeing is not going on, only memory is going on, and my
organism as a whole is not touched.

I had insights as a Christian Scientist, as an atheist, and as a true-believer in Gestalt Therapy. Insights followed, no matter what my premise and no matter what the contradiction. The impact of "seeing the light" has sometimes been so intense that it seemed as though I were experiencing a kind of direct perception of reality. But now I doubt that an insight is a revelation. It is probably not more than an elaboration of my present standpoint.

The danger with insights is that they are
oversimplifications.

No one thing
is more profound
than anything else.

Most of the conversations I hear are carried on as if there really were such a thing as an answer, and as if the people present were actually in possession of it.

I can reverse almost everything I have written and it is equally true.

This turning turning turning of truth
Nothing standing still
And yet the great stillness
and the sameness
The knowing and the never knowing. . . .

They are towing it in now

But when we talked this morning
of things to be
and my friend sailed out
on the smiling waters

I thought I knew

And when the hallowed old woman said
she loved me

I thought I knew

Then she turned her back
and loosened her bowels
and squatted over my friendship

And years ago when he had forsaken
they nodded his praise

and I nodded too
and thought I knew

Now he is in his bottles of death

And once as I thanked the dear
Lord for my wife and child

I thought I knew

And I turned around
and turned again
and only a wordless house

I thought I knew as
I dove into God's shining Truth
I thought I knew

and now I watch my religions
drop from me like a scale

Recently I have felt very pleasant about my occasional
stuttering, and I have actually grown fond of my feelings
of inadequacy and vulnerability. For the first time
in a long while I am beginning to feel quite ordinary and
human, and to be very comfortable around other people,
just as ordinary and imperfect as me.

Tonight I discovered nature. For the first time I saw it.
For the first time I didn't look at it, I listened to it—
not with my ears, although I did that too, but with my
eyes. Instead of pushing out at it, trying to understand
it, I let it speak to me. On my left, some distance away,
was the highway. From there I could hear man—man always
arriving, never quite there. Then I looked at the stars.
They were silent, and powerful beyond all effort. They
were stars being stars and therefore brilliantly alive . . .
how puny are words about stars.

"Gorgeous day isn't it?" "Look at the mist over those
hills." "Isn't that sunset beautiful?" —I wonder why
most of us tack a demand for support on every exclamation
we make about nature . . . or is it that nature is so boundless
that we are always moved to share it?

These leaves are not talking about the "autumn of our lives"; they are talking about our death. And what a startling speech they deliver: Death can be as useful as life, and even more beautiful.

And here comes the finger

of God,

Strumming down this thread

of mountains,

Bringing seven oceans of

black water

inside a single pillow

of

gray

air

I wish I could take my privacy with me. Solitude
instead of isolation. I am on top of this mesa and
still there are a hundred thousand tongues in my head.
Silent *inside*, silent and richly alone . . . then there would
be no need to shun.

the absolute stillness of

moonlight

melting

cloud and field and puddle

into

     abstractions

of perfect peace

I believe that at least one of the reasons why prayer, relaxation drills, yoga, self-hypnotism, tai chi, breathing concentration and Gestalt awareness exercises bring peace and dissolve problems is that they force an end to the merry-go-round of thinking. Either during or after these meditations we do something rare: we stop and *listen*.

stopping

and counting every sound

stopping

and seeing every stone

stopping

and letting in the wind

stopping

and not having to be somebody

In order to listen I will have to listen without obligation,
I will have to give up my *intention* to hear.
If I will let the meaning flow through me like wind
blowing through leaves, then I can open up loosely to
what is being said, instead of howling it down with
my intensity.

The parent who says, "Now you listen to me!" may be
assuring his child's deafness. Recently I have noticed
that if I try to concentrate on what someone is saying,
I can't hear as well as I can if I broaden my awareness
to include more of everything that is going on
around me. When I broaden my awareness, the other
person's words seem to come more slowly.

I can listen to someone without hearing him. Listening is fixing my attention only on the other person. Hearing requires that I listen inside me as I listen to him. Hearing is a rhythm whereby I shuttle between his words and my experience. It includes hearing his entire posture: his eyes, his lips, the tilt of his head, the movement of his fingers. It includes hearing his tone of voice and his silences. And hearing also includes attending to *my* reactions, such as the "sinking feeling" I get when the other person has stopped hearing *me*.

It's not that I don't listen, it's that I listen to something else. As soon as someone starts talking I immediately start thinking—as if their talking were a waste of my time and that now that I have the opportunity to fake it I will do something that is *really* important.

The difference between talking "at" and talking "with" is the difference between touching, and touching and being touched.

There are people I meet (very few) whom I feel close to immediately. Agreeableness does not seem to be a factor. There is in fact a decided absence of striving in their manner—they don't *try* to be friendly, they aren't building anything. I also have the feeling that they are very present: they seem more alert to how I am, and what they notice about me appears in their faces fully and instantly. When these people look at me I have the feeling *I* am being seen. They also seem to know what it is they are saying to me, that is, they seem to hear their own words.

"How am I hearing this person through my arms?" "Am I seeing him with my face?" It is becoming clear to me that I see and hear with my entire body. The tensions in my stomach and back, the position of my head, the movements of my limbs, all affect the quality of my perception. If my legs are crossed and I open them, if I am leaning intently forward and I lean gently back, if my face is tight and I let the muscles go, then a small but measurable change takes place in all the sights and sounds around me.

Last night I was aware that I was using my eyes to signal
Jonas Lions. I was having them do a little act entitled,
"Jonas, I am very interested in what you are saying." I
knew that I was misusing my eyes, but I didn't know how to
stop. Maybe if I had started looking at the details of
his face and posture to see what *else* he was saying. Or
even if I had closed my eyes and noticed how interested
I really was . . . I think that the fear that I am required
to *do something* when people talk gets me into this bind.

Maybe this is a richer way to communicate: to respond to how the other person is *now* instead of to how he is describing himself, what he is telling me he has done or plans to do.

I often get out of balance when I meet someone new, and when René came into the room last night I stopped the light touching of my environment. Maybe next time I will pause to look at all that is going on in the world beside whether or not I am making it with a new stranger.

When I meet someone new I evidently see mostly my projections and very little of the person. If my first impressions are negative, they usually turn out to be inaccurate, and if they are positive, they usually turn out to be incomplete.

I seek no imperfections in the piñon and the pine . . . and none are found.

Sometimes when I meet a person I think is superior
to me, I find myself wanting to be his friend. This kind
of wanting is not love, and its very presence seems to
repulse the other.

I just discovered that what I thought was my desire to
be friends with Ron was really my desire to appease the
neighborhood bully.

What do I do to keep myself from believing that anyone can like me?

I told Nelson that I agreed with his criticism of *Notes* when actually I didn't agree at all. Dishonesty for the sake of appearing honest. What insanity!

Some people are going to like me and some people aren't, so I might as well be me. Then at least I will know that the people who like me, like *me*.

I have lost two friends by being open. I once thought that, if I knew anything, I knew that an honest statement of my feelings leads to greater closeness. And usually it has. But openness can scare the hell out of people. And there are some who take it as hatred. It has been a relief to me to realize that I don't have to act the same way around everyone. I can take people as I find them. I can open my eyes and see what effect my words are having, and if my friend is misunderstanding my intentions, I can drop being that way.

Sometimes a particular friendship is simply not worth all the adjustments I have to make in order to maintain it. And sometimes I meet a man who delights in having enemies and does all he can to add me to his list.

A while back I ran into Elbert and was very hurt that
he didn't seem excited to see me. Later I realized that
I had never especially liked him either.

I don't really know why people react to me the way they
do. Some end up liking me and some don't, and in the
beginning I seldom know which way it will go. Nor does
there seem to be any need to know.

Likes and dislikes are so frequently mutual that expecting
someone to like me when I don't like him is *unrealistic*,
as well as arrogant.

Beulah cut me off and I am still looking for a nice reasonable explanation for why I hate her guts.

Dislike may at times be a signal similar to pain, and pain means "keep away," not "destroy." If I don't like her I do not have to show her unworthy. The question is not "Is she bad?" but "Is she bad for me?"

I suspect that there are many times that I say something critical to a friend, or he does something to annoy me, when our contact has been too prolonged or too intense, and one of us is simply feeling the need for a little time off.

There is an important difference between expressing my antagonism and being critical. When I criticize I say in effect "You are wrong," and I leave unspoken the part I am playing in the condemnation. Criticism is thus "safer" than stating my feelings as mine because the other person will usually respond to the words and not to me. If, however, I say, "This is what goes off in me when you do such-and-such," I am admitting that all criticism requires a criticizer.

So often my confessions are a request for permission: I am testing to see if it will be OK with everyone if I happen to be myself. I tell them what I am like, before I risk being that way.

The effect of flattery is to keep the other person at a distance.

If "guilt is resentment," is adoration a desire for approval?

Expressing anger is a very intimate act. And so, of course, it is very risky. It at once opens me up to a closer relationship, or to a verbal kick in the groin. I was irritated at Hank's denouncing every comment that anyone made at the meeting, but instead of telling him that, I argued against his logic. That was not expressing my irritation, it was reacting to it. Later, when I expressed it directly and told him how mad I was at his attitude, he made a very personal confession of how stupid he felt around all of us. He *could* have come back with a rebuff that would have hurt me.

Again and again I am surprised at how often people appreciate my going to them with my negative feelings. I am afraid that my words will hurt our friendship, but it has turned out that they usually strengthen it.

For seven months I mistook reputation for humanity, politeness for love, being used for being appreciated. For seven months I thought she was my friend . . . and now my hurt and anger at what she has done are making me as petty as she is, and I can't even pretend I am superior.

How can there be pettiness and that sunset on the same planet? Is it possible for me to look at narrowness and cruelty the way I am looking at these clouds? Is there any wonder in the small selfish parts of man?—I certainly see none; it's all in this sky.

Gene told me that last night Beulah criticized me in front of several people. Beulah ate dinner with us the night before and was very friendly. Why didn't she say those words to me? This situation is classic: One friend tells me what another friend said, and I hurt. I am disappointed in the friend who criticizes, and I question the motives of the friend who reports it. Surely there is a way out of this smallness. How do I make myself ache every time this happens?

Recently I have been noticing that what I think I want from someone else is really what I want from myself. For a long time I have been experiencing Jonas as a know-it-all, then the other night Gayle said, "Do you realize that you act like a little boy when you're around him?" Of course! What I wanted was not for Jonas to stop being a know-it-all but for me to stop being a know-nothing. (And what I want is not for Lillith to stop being domineering but for me to start standing up for myself.)

If I don't *need* anything from you, I feel freer to tell you what I *want*.

Other people's traits, if I see them as "faults," tend to draw out the same traits in me. I am controlled by what I experience as "bad" in another person.

Just when I have figured out what I don't like about someone, and what I am going to do about it, I will see him again and he will be different.

I don't want to argue any more about how he "is." You see him one way, I see him another way, he sees himself a third way. Now if you want to talk about what how we see him indicates about us . . .

When I criticize a person I am assuming that he has a choice.

"It's a little thing to do." "You owe her at least that much." "It's your duty." I have never before realized how angry and powerful is this concept of our owing other people until I started saying "no" to my family and friends' requests that I inscribe their copies of Notes. I was at a point in my life where I was reacting strongly against this type of etiquette, but I was not asking that they agree with my position, just that they let me be myself as I found myself then. But all that they were able to see was that I "should" do it because they were "family" or because of "all they had done for me" or because "we had been close for so long."

The working definition of "gratitude" is often: "I have
done many things for you so now by God you can do this for
me." "Do things for" so often translates "give into"
rather than "give." If I *give*, that comes from inside.

"Kindness": "Will you hurry up dammit—I'm standing here
holding the door for you!"

What possible meaning can "I love you" have if it is an
answer?

Oh, I see: You want me to do what I want to do whether I want to do it or not.

Kay said, "I want all the gossiping to end now." I felt encumbered. Now I see that Kay was making a resolution, and I see that I don't have to be bound by someone else's resolution—even if she wants me to.

If I want to make you feel good so that I will feel good, whose interest do I have at heart? If you are feeling bad, will you really be better off if I "make" you feel better?

Last week I realized how often I ask Gayle to do things for me ("While you're up will you . . ."). I saw that I wanted to start doing these things for myself, and since I have begun, I have felt as if I have come together in a more comfortable fit.

Gayle always does the laundry, but today when I decided to do it myself I was surprised at my feeling of panic. I see that I have given up more than just drudgery by not doing for myself.

Living without pressure—without putting it on myself or others—without allowing others to put it on me. Living without strings, or selling, or charming, or kidding into compliance, or manipulating through niceness or threatened anger. Standing in the face of silence, and threats, and expectations, and misunderstandings—standing and gently saying, "No thank you, I'll be myself."

Why in the hell am I still trying to reform my dad?

I cannot disregard my relatives in the name of increased
awareness. Increased awareness is increased awareness.

I strongly object to the way elderly people are shoved
around "for their own good." My grandmother has diabetes,
and if knowing this she chooses to eat chocolates,
that is her business. I would rather die in one year of
candy than in ten of being watched over.

Many "human potential people" talk as if a sensual feeling for another is more *legitimate* than a feeling of loyalty for one's spouse. Queen Victoria is simply standing on her head.

"My" son, "my" wife—does the "my" really bring me closer to them? "Paddlefoot is my horse and I want to take good care of him"—but doesn't "my" sooner or later turn into: "Paddlefoot is my horse and I can treat him any way I want"? Which attitude has more potential closeness and consideration: "my child" or, as the Hopis have it, "the child I live with"?

I say "my wife Gayle," Charlotte says "my friend Gayle,"
Frances says "my daughter Gayle," and *Gayle* remains the
same.

Ted "Bull" Howard races his jeep up and down his ranch
trying to convince himself that he owns it. Maybe some
day he will notice those billion-year mountains laughing
at him.

I went to my first horse race today
and now I want to be rich
and I am very uncomfortable.
"I own it" is the same mental
poverty as "I want it."
The instant I believe that
I own a few things,
I exclude myself from
all the rest.
This strong and
periodic wanting of
mine begins to recede
whenever I remember that
everything is mine
to enjoy in some way,
that anything
outside me is also inside me,
that I live in this earth
and this earth
lives in me.

Now I am doubting that any human being can be free of beliefs and ideals. And I am thinking that, if this is so, I will be in less danger of self-delusion if I will acknowledge what they are. I know that I presently have one belief about people which I have no way of testing. And I know that I like believing it—I like how it brings me down when I think I am better, and how it brings me up whenever I feel less. My belief is that all people have about the same proportion of light and darkness, wisdom and blindness, that only the *ways* differ in which we are nourishing or destructive. I also have an ideal. It is consideration—not as etiquette, but as a type of awareness which feels good, a sweetly flowing step which comes after the realization that "I am not responsible for you."

I was running in the back hills today, and Anthony came out to ride his bike beside me. To him I was not a "stranger," I was a man running by, and as good a person as any to tell that he hoped very much it would snow in three months.

Why is it that on the highway only children stare out of the rear window and wave at me?

Being habitually silent when a "thank you," a "good-by," or a "hello" is expected is as phony as saying these words automatically.

My two dogs are hopelessly phony—they are *always* glad
to see me.

In your struggle to be real, to be centered, to be you,
have you left a place for me?

I don't want to do it
but I want to do it *for you,*
so I will do it.

Wanting to do it for you is no less a want than wanting to do it for me.

I don't want to, but she wants me to——and that counts for something. The question is how much; and this question is equally as insistent as "Am I true to myself?" In fact, it is the same.

How deeply am I willing to pierce another human being in order to satisfy my absolute now? I am not responsible for other people, but I can choose to be careful. I can choose to be . . . and I am knowing right now that I want to.

I could say that if you had been in good shape you wouldn't have hurt when I slugged you in the stomach. I could say that. And I could say that I am not responsible for how you react to my silence, or my words. But because I am a human being I know something about what it is like for you to be human, and this knowledge makes me aware of the possible consequences of my actions.

Today I have seen two people get physically sick from a lack of love while I stood by and did little. I can't force myself to love someone I have no feeling for, but that situation is so rare—what about the 99% of the time that I *could* feel love if I would only let go?

Love itself is not an act of will, but sometimes I need the force of my volition to break with my habitual responses and pass along the love already here.

It was Christmas and I wanted to put my arms around Dad and tell him that I loved him. But I couldn't. Then it was time to go and I started the drive back. I hadn't cried about anything for ten years, and I had to make crying sounds in my throat for over an hour before I could start.

A few months ago I was out walking with a friend of mine who is a Gestalt therapist. A man walking from the other direction smiled at us and said, "How are you doing?" My friend didn't answer. He explained to me that the question was phony since the man didn't know us.

Today Nat drove me through the little Spanish villages of northern New Mexico. He waved and shouted greetings out the window and asked directions in self-taught Spanish. He stopped to chat with shopkeepers and spent several minutes of warm conversation with an old drunk. All day his face has been bright with love for these people, and their liking of him has been immediate. Nat is not yet enlightened enough to have reasoned out the impossibility of spontaneous love, and, although he does not know it, he has taught me one of the most appreciated lessons of my life.

to sway and not
crack
malleable
but not manipulable

a willingness to be
touched
to move off dead center
(but not from my center)
to move and take my center with me
(my strength, my needs, my caring for me)

a willingness to move
to you
and take me
with me

being me
allowing we

it takes such little effort
to reach
in
to another human being

draw a circle around your love
. . . and hate will walk the line

IN THE BEGINNING was the
mist and the dust and the dream.

And I heard a voice walking
in the cool of the burning,
coming before the fire,
calling to me from the midst
of my awareness saying
Who are you?

And I said I am John.
And he said Who are you?
And I said I am John. And he
said Who are you? And I said:
I AM

Then he closed up the
place of me saying You shall be
One.

AND I JOHN was brought forth
in wisdom and waxed fat and
kicked. And my father filled
my head with soft warm primary
colors and I lived in a
wet dream. For I slept with
the church of my father.

And there appeared in me
a great wonder, and I saw a
new All and a new One. For
last and first were passed
away and there was no more
shore.

And I hid my face in the
image of God and the image
of John was consumed.

And a mighty voice said
Let there be law, and lo,
quiet living law encompassed
and gladdened and constituted
all.

And the law was with God.

And I was one with the law so that the law which was God's was my law and I ruled through all time. Past all space.

And since there was only the law, I the law was all things and I the law was alone. I was everywhere and at once. I did all things at rest.

I the law was God.

BUT IT CAME TO PASS that I saw her coming like the sun rises, for it rose within, a liquid in a liquid a sigh within a sigh.

And her shoulders were licked with starlight and eternity was in her eyes and her hair was soft as angel's breath. But her loins were the howling on high.

And I conceived a love
and bore it, and I John saw
that it was good. And the
love multiplied and subdued
me, for I had never loved
before.

AND BEHOLD a round red
thing lay kindling in the face
of the wilderness. And the
voice closed therein said
Take, eat, this is your body.
    And I took it and ate it
up and my mouth was bitter.
But in my belly it was sweet
as honey. And the voice said
Upon your belly you shall go.
    So I filled my bowels
with the east wind and lifted
the burning lid of hell.
    And I John bred worms
and stank and was like the gods.
    For the smell of fire was
on me.

WHEREFORE I woke. And stood
there with God all over my face.
And night said Wipe him off,
your face comes next.

For only in your flesh
will you touch flesh and only
with your ears will you hear.
And if your brain offend you
pluck it out.

AND I JOHN came forth and my
eyes were bound with a napkin
and my body was bound with
graveclothes.

And I took from me the
graveclothes and the napkin
and spat on the ground. And
I washed my eyes with the
earth and filled my ears with
the sounds of day.

And the daysounds said
unto the deaf Why reason ye
and why do you remember?
For truth and purpose are night,
and night is death. And death
is a sleep without waking.

AND AFTER TRUTH before all
intendings when now was
forever and here was farther
than space, Man loved.
and his love was light
and light is life
and life lives
eternal
without
dream
ing

May 1972
Pojoaque, New Mexico